WELCOME TO YOUR HOMEBUYER JOURNAL

THIS JOURNAL BELONGS TO:

_____

Congrats! You've taken the first step and decided to purchase a home!
Use this journal to keep track of your home buying search.
There is a place for you to jot down notes about your mortgage,
the homes that interest you and the ones you want to see in person.
You will also find graph paper, note paper and
a real estate dictionary to help you along the way!

Follow us on Instagram @peechypages

PEECHY PAGES
HOME BUYER JOURNAL

CONTENTS

MY MORTGAGE 4-12

POTENTIAL HOMES 13-34

MY HOME 35-48

RESOURCES 49-64

DICTIONARY 65-72

NOTES 73-80

❤ MY MORTGAGE ❤

*This section is for all your notes about your mortgage,
conversations about your loan, closing costs notes,
Dos and Don'ts for your loan, etc.*

MORTGAGE

_____
_____
_____
_____
_____
_____
_____
_____
_____
_____
_____
_____
_____
_____
_____
_____
_____
_____
_____
_____
_____
_____
_____
_____

DOS and DON'TS

DON'T - just get pre-qualified for a mortgage, get pre-approved.

NOTES + REMINDERS

_____
_____
_____
_____
_____
_____
_____
_____
_____
_____
_____
_____
_____
_____
_____
_____
_____
_____
_____
_____
_____
_____

DOS and DON'TS

DO – house hunt with an experienced and qualified Realtor.

MORTGAGE

NOTES + REMINDERS

DOS and DON'TS

DON'T – leave your current employer. Job history is very important.

MORTGAGE

DOS and DON'TS

DON'T – place untraceable funds into your bank account.

NOTES + REMINDERS

_____
_____
_____
_____
_____
_____
_____
_____
_____
_____
_____
_____
_____
_____
_____
_____
_____
_____
_____
_____
_____
_____
_____
_____

DOS and DON'TS
DO – keep your spending in check.
Stay current and make payments on time.

MORTGAGE

_____

_____

_____

_____

_____

_____

_____

_____

_____

_____

_____

_____

_____

_____

_____

_____

_____

_____

_____

_____

_____

_____

_____

_____

_____

_____

_____

_____

DOS and DON'TS
DON'T – make any big purchases over the next couple of
months or apply for any new debt until after closing.

NOTES + REMINDERS

DOS and DON'TS

DO - keep good records of all your transactions for your loan.

"Home is where one starts from."

– T. S. Eliot

♥THE HOME SEARCH♥

*This section is for keeping track of the homes you want to see
and to fill in details about the houses you go see with your Realtor.
Take notes or just plain cross out the "no thank you" houses.*

HOME SEARCH

Address:

Price:	Taxes:
MLS #:	School District:
#of Bedrooms:	# of Bathrooms:
Square Footage:	Notes:

Second Visit: ☐YES   ☐NO   ☐Make an offer

Address:	MLS #:
Price:	Taxes:
Showing Date:	School District:
#of Bedrooms:	# of Bathrooms:
Square Footage:	Notes:

Second Visit: ☐YES   ☐NO   ☐Make an offer

Address:

Price:	Taxes:
MLS #:	School District:
#of Bedrooms:	# of Bathrooms:
Square Footage:	Notes:

Second Visit: ☐YES   ☐NO   ☐Make an offer

Address:

Price:	Taxes:
MLS #:	School District:
#of Bedrooms:	# of Bathrooms:
Square Footage:	Notes:

Second Visit: ☐YES   ☐NO   ☐Make an offer

HOME SEARCH

Address:

Price: Taxes:

MLS #:   School District:

#of Bedrooms: # of Bathrooms:

Square Footage: Notes:

Second Visit: ☐ YES   ☐ NO   ☐ Make an offer

Address:

Price: Taxes:

MLS #:   School District:

#of Bedrooms: # of Bathrooms:

Square Footage: Notes:

Second Visit: ☐ YES   ☐ NO   ☐ Make an offer

Address: MLS #:

Price: Taxes:

Showing Date: School District:

#of Bedrooms: # of Bathrooms:

Square Footage: Notes:

Second Visit: ☐ YES   ☐ NO   ☐ Make an offer

Address:

Price: Taxes:

MLS #:   School District:

#of Bedrooms: # of Bathrooms:

Square Footage: Notes:

Second Visit: ☐ YES   ☐ NO   ☐ Make an offer

HOME SEARCH

Address:

Price: Taxes:

MLS #:   School District:

#of Bedrooms: # of Bathrooms:

Square Footage: Notes:

Second Visit: ☐ YES   ☐ NO   ☐ Make an offer

Address: MLS #:

Price: Taxes:

Showing Date: School District:

#of Bedrooms: # of Bathrooms:

Square Footage: Notes:

Second Visit: ☐ YES   ☐ NO   ☐ Make an offer

Address:

Price: Taxes:

MLS #:   School District:

#of Bedrooms: # of Bathrooms:

Square Footage: Notes:

Second Visit: ☐ YES   ☐ NO   ☐ Make an offer

Address:

Price: Taxes:

MLS #:   School District:

#of Bedrooms: # of Bathrooms:

Square Footage: Notes:

Second Visit: ☐ YES   ☐ NO   ☐ Make an offer

HOME SEARCH

Address:

Price: | Taxes:

MLS #: | School District:

#of Bedrooms: | # of Bathrooms:

Square Footage: | Notes:

Second Visit:　☐YES　☐NO　☐Make an offer

Address:

Price: | Taxes:

MLS #: | School District:

#of Bedrooms: | # of Bathrooms:

Square Footage: | Notes:

Second Visit:　☐YES　☐NO　☐Make an offer

Address: | MLS #:

Price: | Taxes:

Showing Date: | School District:

#of Bedrooms: | # of Bathrooms:

Square Footage: | Notes:

Second Visit:　☐YES　☐NO　☐Make an offer

Address:

Price: | Taxes:

MLS #: | School District:

#of Bedrooms: | # of Bathrooms:

Square Footage: | Notes:

Second Visit:　☐YES　☐NO　☐Make an offer

HOME SEARCH

Address:

Price: Taxes:

MLS #:   School District:

#of Bedrooms: # of Bathrooms:

Square Footage: Notes:

Second Visit: ☐ YES   ☐ NO   ☐ Make an offer

Address: MLS #:

Price: Taxes:

Showing Date: School District:

#of Bedrooms: # of Bathrooms:

Square Footage: Notes:

Second Visit: ☐ YES   ☐ NO   ☐ Make an offer

Address:

Price: Taxes:

MLS #:   School District:

#of Bedrooms: # of Bathrooms:

Square Footage: Notes:

Second Visit: ☐ YES   ☐ NO   ☐ Make an offer

Address:

Price: Taxes:

MLS #:   School District:

#of Bedrooms: # of Bathrooms:

Square Footage: Notes:

Second Visit: ☐ YES   ☐ NO   ☐ Make an offer

HOME SEARCH

Address:

Price:	Taxes:
MLS #:	School District:
#of Bedrooms:	# of Bathrooms:
Square Footage:	Notes:

Second Visit: ☐ YES   ☐ NO   ☐ Make an offer

Address:

Price:	Taxes:
MLS #:	School District:
#of Bedrooms:	# of Bathrooms:
Square Footage:	Notes:

Second Visit: ☐ YES   ☐ NO   ☐ Make an offer

Address:	MLS #:
Price:	Taxes:
Showing Date:	School District:
#of Bedrooms:	# of Bathrooms:
Square Footage:	Notes:

Second Visit: ☐ YES   ☐ NO   ☐ Make an offer

Address:

Price:	Taxes:
MLS #:	School District:
#of Bedrooms:	# of Bathrooms:
Square Footage:	Notes:

Second Visit: ☐ YES   ☐ NO   ☐ Make an offer

HOME SEARCH

Address:

Price: Taxes:

MLS #:   School District:

#of Bedrooms: # of Bathrooms:

Square Footage: Notes:

Second Visit: ☐ YES   ☐ NO   ☐ Make an offer

Address: MLS #:

Price: Taxes:

Showing Date: School District:

#of Bedrooms: # of Bathrooms:

Square Footage: Notes:

Second Visit: ☐ YES   ☐ NO   ☐ Make an offer

Address:

Price: Taxes:

MLS #:   School District:

#of Bedrooms: # of Bathrooms:

Square Footage: Notes:

Second Visit: ☐ YES   ☐ NO   ☐ Make an offer

Address:

Price: Taxes:

MLS #:   School District:

#of Bedrooms: # of Bathrooms:

Square Footage: Notes:

Second Visit: ☐ YES   ☐ NO   ☐ Make an offer

HOME SEARCH

Address:

Price: | Taxes:

MLS #: | School District:

#of Bedrooms: | # of Bathrooms:

Square Footage: | Notes:

Second Visit: ☐ YES ☐ NO | ☐ Make an offer

Address:

Price: | Taxes:

MLS #: | School District:

#of Bedrooms: | # of Bathrooms:

Square Footage: | Notes:

Second Visit: ☐ YES ☐ NO | ☐ Make an offer

Address: | MLS #:

Price: | Taxes:

Showing Date: | School District:

#of Bedrooms: | # of Bathrooms:

Square Footage: | Notes:

Second Visit: ☐ YES ☐ NO | ☐ Make an offer

Address:

Price: | Taxes:

MLS #: | School District:

#of Bedrooms: | # of Bathrooms:

Square Footage: | Notes:

Second Visit: ☐ YES ☐ NO | ☐ Make an offer

HOME SEARCH

Address:

Price: Taxes:

MLS #:   School District:

#of Bedrooms: # of Bathrooms:

Square Footage: Notes:

Second Visit: ☐ YES   ☐ NO   ☐ Make an offer

Address: MLS #:

Price: Taxes:

Showing Date: School District:

#of Bedrooms: # of Bathrooms:

Square Footage: Notes:

Second Visit: ☐ YES   ☐ NO   ☐ Make an offer

Address:

Price: Taxes:

MLS #:   School District:

#of Bedrooms: # of Bathrooms:

Square Footage: Notes:

Second Visit: ☐ YES   ☐ NO   ☐ Make an offer

Address:

Price: Taxes:

MLS #:   School District:

#of Bedrooms: # of Bathrooms:

Square Footage: Notes:

Second Visit: ☐ YES   ☐ NO   ☐ Make an offer

HOME SEARCH

Address:

Price:	Taxes:
MLS #:	School District:
#of Bedrooms:	# of Bathrooms:
Square Footage:	Notes:

Second Visit: ☐ YES ☐ NO   ☐ Make an offer

Address:

Price:	Taxes:
MLS #:	School District:
#of Bedrooms:	# of Bathrooms:
Square Footage:	Notes:

Second Visit: ☐ YES ☐ NO   ☐ Make an offer

Address:	MLS #:
Price:	Taxes:
Showing Date:	School District:
#of Bedrooms:	# of Bathrooms:
Square Footage:	Notes:

Second Visit: ☐ YES ☐ NO   ☐ Make an offer

Address:

Price:	Taxes:
MLS #:	School District:
#of Bedrooms:	# of Bathrooms:
Square Footage:	Notes:

Second Visit: ☐ YES ☐ NO   ☐ Make an offer

HOME SEARCH

Address:

Price:	Taxes:
MLS #:	School District:
#of Bedrooms:	# of Bathrooms:
Square Footage:	Notes:

Second Visit: ☐ YES   ☐ NO   ☐ Make an offer

Address:	MLS #:
Price:	Taxes:
Showing Date:	School District:
#of Bedrooms:	# of Bathrooms:
Square Footage:	Notes:

Second Visit: ☐ YES   ☐ NO   ☐ Make an offer

Address:

Price:	Taxes:
MLS #:	School District:
#of Bedrooms:	# of Bathrooms:
Square Footage:	Notes:

Second Visit: ☐ YES   ☐ NO   ☐ Make an offer

Address:

Price:	Taxes:
MLS #:	School District:
#of Bedrooms:	# of Bathrooms:
Square Footage:	Notes:

Second Visit: ☐ YES   ☐ NO   ☐ Make an offer

HOME SEARCH

Address:

Price: Taxes:

MLS #:   School District:

#of Bedrooms: # of Bathrooms:

Square Footage: Notes:

Second Visit: ☐ YES   ☐ NO   ☐ Make an offer

Address:

Price: Taxes:

MLS #:   School District:

#of Bedrooms: # of Bathrooms:

Square Footage: Notes:

Second Visit: ☐ YES   ☐ NO   ☐ Make an offer

Address: MLS #:

Price: Taxes:

Showing Date: School District:

#of Bedrooms: # of Bathrooms:

Square Footage: Notes:

Second Visit: ☐ YES   ☐ NO   ☐ Make an offer

Address:

Price: Taxes:

MLS #:   School District:

#of Bedrooms: # of Bathrooms:

Square Footage: Notes:

Second Visit: ☐ YES   ☐ NO   ☐ Make an offer

HOME SEARCH

Address:

Price:	Taxes:
MLS #:	School District:
#of Bedrooms:	# of Bathrooms:
Square Footage:	Notes:
Second Visit: ☐ YES ☐ NO	☐ Make an offer

Address:	MLS #:
Price:	Taxes:
Showing Date:	School District:
#of Bedrooms:	# of Bathrooms:
Square Footage:	Notes:
Second Visit: ☐ YES ☐ NO	☐ Make an offer

Address:

Price:	Taxes:
MLS #:	School District:
#of Bedrooms:	# of Bathrooms:
Square Footage:	Notes:
Second Visit: ☐ YES ☐ NO	☐ Make an offer

Address:

Price:	Taxes:
MLS #:	School District:
#of Bedrooms:	# of Bathrooms:
Square Footage:	Notes:
Second Visit: ☐ YES ☐ NO	☐ Make an offer

HOME SEARCH

Address:

Price:	Taxes:
MLS #:	School District:
#of Bedrooms:	# of Bathrooms:
Square Footage:	Notes:

Second Visit: ☐ YES   ☐ NO   ☐ Make an offer

Address:

Price:	Taxes:
MLS #:	School District:
#of Bedrooms:	# of Bathrooms:
Square Footage:	Notes:

Second Visit: ☐ YES   ☐ NO   ☐ Make an offer

Address:	MLS #:
Price:	Taxes:
Showing Date:	School District:
#of Bedrooms:	# of Bathrooms:
Square Footage:	Notes:

Second Visit: ☐ YES   ☐ NO   ☐ Make an offer

Address:

Price:	Taxes:
MLS #:	School District:
#of Bedrooms:	# of Bathrooms:
Square Footage:	Notes:

Second Visit: ☐ YES   ☐ NO   ☐ Make an offer

HOME SEARCH

Address:	
Price:	Taxes:
MLS #:	School District:
#of Bedrooms:	# of Bathrooms:
Square Footage:	Notes:
Second Visit: ☐ YES ☐ NO	☐ Make an offer

Address:	MLS #:
Price:	Taxes:
Showing Date:	School District:
#of Bedrooms:	# of Bathrooms:
Square Footage:	Notes:
Second Visit: ☐ YES ☐ NO	☐ Make an offer

Address:	
Price:	Taxes:
MLS #:	School District:
#of Bedrooms:	# of Bathrooms:
Square Footage:	Notes:
Second Visit: ☐ YES ☐ NO	☐ Make an offer

Address:	
Price:	Taxes:
MLS #:	School District:
#of Bedrooms:	# of Bathrooms:
Square Footage:	Notes:
Second Visit: ☐ YES ☐ NO	☐ Make an offer

HOME SEARCH

Address:

Price: Taxes:

MLS #:   School District:

#of Bedrooms: # of Bathrooms:

Square Footage: Notes:

Second Visit: ☐ YES   ☐ NO   ☐ Make an offer

Address:

Price: Taxes:

MLS #:   School District:

#of Bedrooms: # of Bathrooms:

Square Footage: Notes:

Second Visit: ☐ YES   ☐ NO   ☐ Make an offer

Address: MLS #:

Price: Taxes:

Showing Date: School District:

#of Bedrooms: # of Bathrooms:

Square Footage: Notes:

Second Visit: ☐ YES   ☐ NO   ☐ Make an offer

Address:

Price: Taxes:

MLS #:   School District:

#of Bedrooms: # of Bathrooms:

Square Footage: Notes:

Second Visit: ☐ YES   ☐ NO   ☐ Make an offer

HOME SEARCH

NOTES + REMINDERS

HOME SEARCH

NOTES + REMINDERS

"A man travels the world over in
search of what he needs and
returns home to find it."
- George A. Moore

❤ MY HOME ❤

*Use this section for inspection notes, paint colors and
things to remember once you leave the house
and don't see it again until closing.*

MY HOME: NOTES + REMINDERS

MY HOME: NOTES + REMINDERS

MY HOME: NOTES + REMINDERS

MY HOME: NOTES + REMINDERS

MY HOME: NOTES + REMINDERS

MY HOME: NOTES + REMINDERS

MY HOME: NOTES + REMINDERS

MY HOME: NOTES + REMINDERS

MY HOME: NOTES + REMINDERS

_____
_____
_____
_____
_____

MY HOME: NOTES + REMINDERS

MY HOME: NOTES + REMINDERS

MY HOME: NOTES + REMINDERS

"A house is made with
walls and beams. A home is
made with love and dreams."
– Unknown

♥ RESOURCES ♥

Use this section to write down referrals for contractors,
inspectors and anyone house-related that you may need.

RESOURCES

Company:

Website:

Contact:

Phone:

Email:

Appointment:

Notes + Reminders:

_____

_____

_____

_____

_____

Company:

Website:

Contact:

Phone:

Email:

Appointment:

Notes + Reminders:

_____

_____

_____

_____

_____

RESOURCES

Company:

Website:

Contact:

Phone:

Email:

Appointment:

Notes + Reminders:

_____

_____

_____

_____

_____

Company:

Website:

Contact:

Phone:

Email:

Appointment:

Notes + Reminders:

_____

_____

_____

_____

_____

RESOURCES

Company:

Website:

Contact:

Phone:

Email:

Appointment:

Notes + Reminders:

_____

_____

_____

_____

_____

_____

Company:

Website:

Contact:

Phone:

Email:

Appointment:

Notes + Reminders:

_____

_____

_____

_____

_____

_____

RESOURCES

Company:

Website:

Contact:

Phone:

Email:

Appointment:

Notes + Reminders:

_____

_____

_____

_____

_____

Company:

Website:

Contact:

Phone:

Email:

Appointment:

Notes + Reminders:

_____

_____

_____

_____

_____

RESOURCES

Company:

Website:

Contact:

Phone:

Email:

Appointment:

Notes + Reminders:

_____

_____

_____

_____

_____

Company:

Website:

Contact:

Phone:

Email:

Appointment:

Notes + Reminders:

_____

_____

_____

_____

_____

RESOURCES

Company:

Website:

Contact:

Phone:

Email:

Appointment:

Notes + Reminders:

Company:

Website:

Contact:

Phone:

Email:

Appointment:

Notes + Reminders:

RESOURCES

Company:

Website:

Contact:

Phone:

Email:

Appointment:

Notes + Reminders:

_____

_____

_____

_____

_____

Company:

Website:

Contact:

Phone:

Email:

Appointment:

Notes + Reminders:

_____

_____

_____

_____

_____

RESOURCES

Company:

Website:

Contact:

Phone:

Email:

Appointment:

Notes + Reminders:

_____

_____

_____

_____

_____

Company:

Website:

Contact:

Phone:

Email:

Appointment:

Notes + Reminders:

_____

_____

_____

_____

_____

RESOURCES

Company:

Website:

Contact:

Phone:

Email:

Appointment:

Notes + Reminders:

_____

_____

_____

_____

_____

Company:

Website:

Contact:

Phone:

Email:

Appointment:

Notes + Reminders:

_____

_____

_____

_____

_____

RESOURCES

Company:

Website:

Contact:

Phone:

Email:

Appointment:

Notes + Reminders:

Company:

Website:

Contact:

Phone:

Email:

Appointment:

Notes + Reminders:

RESOURCES: NOTES + REMINDERS

RESOURCES: NOTES + REMINDERS

RESOURCES: NOTES + REMINDERS

RESOURCES: NOTES + REMINDERS

"The ache for home lives in all of us,
the safe place where we can go
as we are and not be questioned."
- Maya Angelou

HOMEBUYER'S DICTIONARY

Must-know terms for every stage of buying a home.

STAGE 1: PREPARE YOUR FINANCES

Annual income - Money you receive over the course of a year, whether it's from wages or salary, alimony or child support, rental payments, commissions, investments or other sources.

Conforming loan - A mortgage loan that meets guidelines established by Fannie Mae and Fredie Mac and falls below a loan amount specified by the Federal Housing Finance Agency. In 2019, that amount was $484,350 for a single-family home in most of the U.S.

Debt-to-income ratio (DTI) - One way to measure your ability to repay debt, DTI is the comparison of your monthly debt payments to your monthly income before taxes, expressed as a percentage. Many mortgage lenders prefer this figure, including a mortgage payment, to be no higher than 36 percent.

Down payment - The amount of cash you can put toward the purchase price of a home. Down payments often range from 3 to 20 percent of the home price.

Loan-to-value ratio (LTV) -The total amount of your mortgage compared to the home's appraised value, expressed as a percentage. If your down payment is less than 20 percent of the purchase price, your LTV is above 80 percent, so you generally pay a higher interest rate on your mortgage and may need to pay private mortgage insurance (PMI).

STAGE 2: GET PREQUALIFY WITH THE RIGHT LOAN

Loan Estimate (LE) - A disclosure to help consumers understand the key loan terms and estimated costs of a mortgage. After a consumer submits six key elements - name, income, Social Security number, property address, estimated property value and desired loan amount - the lender is required to provide this form. All lenders are required to use the same standard Loan Estimate form to make it easier for consumers to compare and shop for a mortgage.

Preapproval - A lender's conditional agreement to lend you a specific amount of money, made after confirming your financial information such as income and assets. Conditions may include a home appraisal and no significant changes to your finances.

Prequalification - When a lender estimates in advance how much you can borrow to buy a home, based on financial and other information (such as employment history) that you provide. It is not a commitment to lend, and you will need to submit additional information for review and approval.

PITI - An acronym for principal, interest, taxes and insurance. Sometimes called your monthly housing expense, it includes your mortgage payment and a monthly portion of your real estate taxes and homeowners insurance.

PMI - An acronym for private mortgage insurance, which protects the lender against losses if you cannot repay your loan. Your lender may require it if your down payment is less than 20 percent.

STAGE 3: PICK YOUR PROPERTY + GET YOUR OFFER ACCEPTED

Comps - Short for "comparables." These are recently sold properties similar to the home you want, with approximately the same size, location and amenities. They help an appraiser determine a property's fair market value.

Contingencies - Conditions in a sales contract that must be satisfied before the home sale can occur. Some common contingencies: The appraised value must support the sales price, the house must pass inspection, and the borrower must be approved for a loan. Others might require a check for termites or the sale of the buyer's current home.

Inspection - A visual and mechanical examination of a home to identify defects and assess the home's condition.

STAGE 4: HOLD ON THROUGH THE MORTGAGE PROCESS

Appraisal - An informed estimate of a home's value, generally done by an independent, professional licensed appraiser and typically required and ordered by the lender in conjunction with the mortgage application.

Closing costs - Also known as settlement costs, these are the costs incurred when getting a mortgage. They might include attorney fees, preparation and title search fees, discount points, appraisal fees, title insurance and credit report charges. They are typically 2 to 5 percent of your loan amount and are often paid at closing or just before.

Escrow - Funds deposited with a third party and held until a specific date is reached and/or a specific condition is met. For example, when you make an offer on a home, your earnest money deposit may be held in an escrow account until closing. Some lenders may require borrowers to establish an escrow account at closing comprised of future tax and insurance payments. The loan servicer then makes your property tax and insurance payments on your behalf.

Mortgage points (or discount points) - An amount paid to the lender, typically at closing, to lower (or buy down) the interest rate if the buyer chooses to do so. One discount point equals one percentage point of the loan amount. For example, 2 points on a $100,000 mortgage cost $2,000.

Origination fee - A fee from the lender that covers expenses of processing a mortgage loan. It is usually a percentage of the amount loaned

- often 1 percent. It can be expressed in the form of points or a flat fee.

Title insurance - Insurance that protects against issues, such as a tax lien or other legal claim, that would affect ownership of the property.

Underwriting - The lender reviews submitted documents to verify the borrower's finances and other factors related to the home, such as the title search and appraisal, then decides to approve or deny the loan.

STAGE 5: CLOSING - YOUR ALMOST HOME

Closing - The last step of homebuying, also called the settlement. You sign all the necessary documents to finalize the sale and take responsibility for the mortgage loan.

Closing Disclosure (CD) - A document that provides key information about your loan, such as the interest rate, monthly payments and closing costs. The lender must give you this document at least three business days before you close on the loan, and the information should match the Loan Estimate you received when you applied.

Deed - A document that legally transfers ownership of real estate.

Definitions provided by **Better Money Habits**®

"Yes, your home is your castle,
but it is also your identity and your
possibility to be open to others."
- David Soul

"I want my home to be that kind
of place –a place of sustenance,
a place of invitation,
a place of welcome."
– Mary DeMuth

NOTES

NOTES

NOTES

NOTES

NOTES

NOTES

NOTES

"Where we love is home
- home that our feet may leave,
but not our hearts."
-Oliver Wendell Holmes, Sr.

CPSIA information can be obtained
at www.ICGtesting.com
Printed in the USA
LVHW080239191219
641043LV00010B/662/P